BRILLIANT MINDS

SHANNON MEYERKORT
AMY BLACKWELL

affirm press

Contents

For parents and teachers

If you're reading this, you might have a young person in your life who has recently received a dyslexia diagnosis or who may have undiagnosed dyslexia. Dyslexia is a neurological condition affecting a person's ability to read and write. It is unrelated to intelligence and does not discriminate by gender, socioeconomic status or ethnicity. Dyslexia is thought to affect at least one in every ten people in Australia, which means there are more than 400,000 children with dyslexia – diagnosed or not – in Australian schools.

Despite the fact that so many schoolchildren (and adults) have dyslexia, very few books highlight the many incredible role models who live with dyslexia and talk about their challenges and their achievements in an affirming and accessible way for younger readers.

When my youngest daughter, Mia-Rose, was diagnosed with dyslexia a few years ago, I could not find a single book that would give her dyslexic role models and fill her with encouragement, confidence and hope for her future. I realised I would need to write the book myself.

Brilliant Minds: 30 Dyslexic Heroes Who Changed Our World is precisely the book I wish I had found on the shelves in those early days. It doesn't shy away from the fact that the school years are tough and that kids with dyslexia will struggle, but it paints a picture of hope, because every person in this book discovered something important about themselves through their struggles with reading and writing.

The people featured in this book come from different walks of life and have pursued very different careers. But they have a few things in common, which is likely a result of their dyslexia. Some of these assets include creative problem-solving skills; a unique ability to see the bigger picture; coping mechanisms that allow them to adapt, to prioritise their strengths and find ways to manage their weaknesses; and a tenacious drive to keep going, even when the odds feel stacked against them.

Not every child with dyslexia will go on to be a prime minister or to win an Academy Award. But then again, nor will every child who doesn't have dyslexia. This book is not meant to add more stress and obligation to kids who are already working so incredibly hard, but I do hope it gives children, teachers and parents the reassurance that dyslexia will not prevent them from reaching their potential.

Shannon Meyerkort

For kids

Being diagnosed with dyslexia can be a little scary at the start, but you just have to believe in yourself. You may need lots of help, which can feel hard and a bit boring, but it's worth it.

Don't think of yourself as someone who *won't* achieve but as someone who *can* achieve if you put your mind to it. Remember, you have lots of people on your team (including the person who gave you this book) – they're on your side.

You can still be brilliant without being one of these people in this book. Be you and make small steps. Make yourself happy and you will make others happy.

Mia-Rose Meyerkort

Dav Pilkey

Author and Illustrator

Born 4 March 1966 • USA

'Try to remember that being unsuccessful in school doesn't automatically mean you'll be unsuccessful in life. Lots of people who didn't excel in school still went on to have successful lives.'

Dav Pilkey

Dav always liked making people laugh. He described himself as the class clown at school, and the kids in his class thought he was very funny. Dav found it difficult to stay still and quiet in class because he had ADHD. He also had dyslexia, which made reading and writing very hard for him. His primary school teachers didn't understand. They thought he was a troublemaker and would send him out of the classroom to sit by himself in the hall.

When Dav was feeling bored by himself in the hall, he would staple sheets of paper together to make a book. Most of the books that he could read from the school library were for little kids. But soon he discovered comic books, which were for older kids and had pictures to give clues about what the words meant. Dav knew he was really good at drawing, so he was inspired to start making his own comic books.

One day, Dav's Grade 2 teacher said the word 'underwear' and everyone sniggered and snorted; some kids even rolled around on the floor laughing. Dav realised that talking about underwear was funny, and so he created a character who wears white undies and a red cape. Dav called him Captain Underpants and made him the star of a new comic book, but Dav's teacher took his book and tore it up, telling him he could not spend his life writing silly stories.

Dav didn't listen, and he continued writing and drawing his comics. Even when it was hard, Dav knew that reading and writing gave him superpowers, such as the power to travel to incredible places in his mind and the power to make people laugh.

Dav's parents were very supportive, and he ended up going to university, where he studied English. One day, Dav's professor asked to see what Dav had been drawing in his notebook. But Dav didn't get in trouble this time! The professor told him how good his stories were and recommended that he turn them into a real book for children.

Dav was only 19 years old when he had his first book published. Today, Dav's books have sold over 80 million copies! They've been translated into 20 languages and made into a movie and TV shows.

Being dyslexic has not stopped Dav from being a successful author. Being told 'no' certainly didn't stop Dav from creating more stories. Even *Captain Underpants* being one of the most banned books in the world did not stop him from carrying on. He remembers what it was like to find reading difficult and boring as a child, and nothing will stop him from writing fun books that kids want to read.

Just like me

Jerry Pinkney – Author and illustrator

Liz Pichon – Author and illustrator

Ann Bancroft

Polar Explorer

Born 29 September 1955 • USA

'I don't know anyone with dyslexia who would change [themselves]. It's been a great asset.'

Ann Bancroft

Ann grew up in rural Minnesota as part of a family who loved physical activities like canoeing and camping. Ann loved being outdoors and taking risks. By the age of eight, she was organising adventures with friends, like camping in the backyard – even in the middle of winter, when it would often drop to below freezing! But Ann didn't mind the cold; her dream was to go to the North Pole.

Thanks to all of the outdoor activities that Ann and her family did, she was very athletic and excelled at sports. But this was the opposite of how she performed academically. She struggled with reading, spelling and maths. Her grades were poor, even when she had extra tutoring. By Year 7, Ann's teachers suggested she get tested for dyslexia.

Ann's parents were relieved to learn she had dyslexia, but for Ann it was horrible to feel different from the other kids. As a teenager, she just wanted to fit in. In the 1960s, there were no special education classes for dyslexia. Ann kept falling behind at school, even with tutoring and summer school. Ann was even removed from the few classes she loved – like sport, music and art – and made to spend the extra time studying. No one realised how important it was for Ann to do the subjects where she excelled and had the chance to shine. These activities were Ann's passion, and doing them made her feel like she could be herself.

But all of Ann's hard work paid off: she went to university and graduated as a sports and special education teacher with a love of the great outdoors.

Ann built a reputation as an adventurer and four years later, she was invited to join a special expedition to the North Pole. In 1986, at the age of 31, Ann became the first woman to reach the North Pole after walking and dog-sledding more than 1,600 kilometres over 56 days with a team of 7 men and 49 dogs.

Seven years later, she led an expedition to the South Pole, joined by other female explorers. This made Ann the first woman to cross the ice to both the North Pole and the South Pole.

Ann believes that her dyslexia and the years of effort she put in at school were the perfect training for becoming a polar explorer. She said that expedition people focus on one step at a time, and that it's about hard work rather than being the fastest.

Ann established the Bancroft Foundation to help other girls find their place in the world. She believes it's important for children to have access to their own lifeblood activities – where they excel and feel empowered – and she wants to inspire others to follow their dreams, just like she did.

Just like me

Dr Robert Ballard – Marine explorer

Ansel Adams – Photographer and environmentalist

Muhammad Ali

Champion Boxer

Born 17 January 1942 • USA

Died 3 June 2016 • USA

'If my mind can conceive it, and I can believe it — then I can achieve it.'

ALI

Muhammad Ali

Muhammad Ali was born with the name Cassius Clay and grew up in a large family in Kentucky. When he was 12, a thief stole his bike. Cassius ran to the local police station in tears to tell them what happened, saying he wanted to hit the person who stole his bike. The police officer spoke to the upset boy. He said that before Cassius could go chasing thieves and threatening to hit them, perhaps he should learn how to box.

Before long, Cassius was training to become a boxer. He was much better at boxing than he was at school. Cassius struggled to read and write and got very bad grades. His teachers called him 'dumb', but Cassius knew he had other strengths. He had enough belief in himself to know that he would achieve great things.

In 1960, when Cassius was still only 18, he won a gold medal at the Olympic Games. This set him on the path to become a professional boxer. He converted to Islam the following year and changed his name to Muhammad Ali, which means 'beloved of God'. Muhammad Ali had strong political beliefs and refused to fight in the Vietnam War. He was always working to improve the lives of African Americans. He donated many millions of dollars to charity and helped people of all religious backgrounds.

Muhammad Ali is regarded as one of the most important sportspeople of the 20th century and the greatest boxer of all time.

But as someone who grew up being called 'dumb', he was aware of how labels could impact a child's self-esteem, even long after they left school. It wasn't until he was older that he found out that he had dyslexia. As an adult, he had a new fight – making sure that kids learned to read and stayed engaged at school.

And because Muhammad Ali also knew that dyslexia could affect kids' love of reading, especially if the books were too hard or boring, he created a series of books that would help young readers who were struggling to read. As the father of a dyslexic daughter, he was even more motivated to change how people view learning differences.

Muhammad Ali did what he could to empower kids to overcome their challenges and inspire them to believe that they could do great things, too.

Just like me

Magic Johnson – Basketballer

Kobe Bryant – Basketballer

Jessica Watson

Solo Sailor

Born 18 May 1993 • Australia

'I've learned that anyone can choose to manage their fears and develop the resilience to overcome setbacks and reach the smaller milestones that enable you to achieve big, audacious goals.'

ella's
pink lady

Jessica Watson

When Jessica was 11, her mum read her a story about Jesse Martin, who had sailed around the world all by himself at the age of 18. Even though Jessica was old enough to read independently, her mum still read to her. This was because Jessica had severe dyslexia. Jessica thought that if Jesse, who was just an ordinary kid like she was, could do something incredible like sail around the world, then maybe she could do something amazing, too.

Together with her brother and sisters, Jessica had been taking sailing lessons since she was a child. Inspired by Jesse's story, Jessica set herself a bold new goal. She spent the next few years training, developing skills and earning qualifications. After going on lots of smaller journeys, Jessica finally convinced her parents to let her sail around the Southern Hemisphere.

The journey took seven months, and she sailed nearly 23,000 nautical miles around the world on her own in a little pink boat. She wrote a blog and kept in contact with her family by phone, but otherwise she was completely alone. Some days she would see shooting stars or animals like a blue whale or a pod of dolphins, while other days she had to battle terrible storms that knocked over her boat. Sometimes she baked bread, but the rest of the time Jessica survived on tinned food and dried fruit.

When Jessica sailed back into Sydney Harbour at the end of her journey, she was only 16 years old, making her the youngest person to ever sail around the world solo and unassisted. The prime minister of Australia was waiting to greet the boat when Jessica arrived and called her an Australian hero. Jessica politely disagreed, saying she was just an ordinary person who worked hard to achieve her dream.

Jessica's dyslexia did not stop her from attempting her record-breaking adventure – it made her more determined to succeed. She wanted to show people you can be extraordinary even if you have difficulties. Two years after returning from her journey, Jessica received an Order of Australia medal for her services to sailing and youth.

Jessica is now in her late twenties and has achieved many more great things that people might not have thought possible for her, like having a book published, starting a marine company, studying a Master of Business Administration, and being a representative for the United Nations World Food Programme.

She has proven to others that just because you have difficulty spelling, it doesn't mean you can't break frontiers.

Just like me

Paul Elvstrøm – Olympic sailor

David Pescud – Sailor and founder of Sailors with DisABILITIES

Dr Jack Horner

Palaeontologist

Born 15 June 1946 • USA

'Personally, I think dyslexia and the consequences of dyslexia – learning to deal with failure – explain my own success. From my failures, I've learned where I need help, such as in reading and math. But I've also learned from my accomplishments what I'm better at than the linear thinkers.'

Dr Jack Horner

When Jack was growing up, he had two dreams: to have a pet dinosaur and to be a palaeontologist – a scientist who studies dinosaurs.

From a very young age, Jack's mum and dad would drive him out to dig sites, where people were searching for fossils. Jack was only 8 years old when he discovered his first dinosaur bone. By the age of 12, he had built a fossil exhibit at the local library.

Jack is a spatial thinker. This means he thinks in images rather than words and tends to understand a concept all at once, rather than in step-by-step details. His brain is very good at making connections that other people can't see.

All of this helped Jack to excel at science, but he found other parts of school difficult. He was slow at reading and writing and found maths challenging. The other kids didn't understand Jack's difficulties and called him 'dumb', so he preferred to play by himself. It was a lonely time for Jack.

Though Jack was not performing well at school, his parents always encouraged his special interests and big ideas. During high school, he built some very impressive science projects, like a working rocket and a generator. In his senior year, his project on comparing fossils from different regions in North America won the top prize in the State Fair and also caught the eye of one the judges, who encouraged Jack to enrol at the University of Montana.

After failing each of his classes, Jack left the university. If he wanted to become a palaeontologist, he would need to find another way to fulfil his dream. He wrote to all the museums he could think of and was eventually offered a job as a technician at the Princeton University Natural History Museum.

It was during this time that Jack discovered he had dyslexia. It didn't make reading any easier, but at least he understood why he thought and learned differently from other people.

Jack's brilliant ideas meant he was always at the forefront of research. He realised that dinosaurs were sociable and lived in herds. He was the first person to discover nests of dinosaur eggs in North America. And because he was willing to take risks that others were not, he was also the first person to crack open a fossilised egg to see the dinosaur embryo inside it.

One day, Jack received a call from Steven Spielberg, the famous director (who also has dyslexia). Steven asked if Jack would help with his new film, *Jurassic Park*. Steven wanted to model the palaeontologist character on Jack.

Just like in the movie, one of Jack's recent projects is trying to create his own dinosaur from a chicken embryo. So, maybe one day Jack will have achieved *both* his childhood dreams.

Just like me

Jacques Dubochet – Biochemist and Nobel Prize winner

Imaan Javan – Business leader and scientist

Erna Solberg

Prime Minister

Born 24 January 1961 • Norway

'I am dyslexic and I write it myself.'

Erna Solberg

When Erna was growing up in Norway with her two siblings, there was always lively debate and discussion around the kitchen table. Erna's father wanted the children to understand politics and what was happening in the world. He wanted them to know that there were always things to consider beyond their own lives.

Erna was glad to think outside of her own life because she was having a difficult time at school. Her teachers said she wrote poorly and gave her bad grades. When she was 16, she was identified as having dyslexia.

Erna did not let this stop her. She was popular with the other students, and even though her teachers complained she talked too much, Erna found it easy to lead discussions and take charge. These leadership attributes spurred Erna to become involved in student politics and she was soon elected to the School Student Union of Norway. Erna took this role seriously and worked hard at it. She found herself very busy with things like organising a national charity event and becoming a Girl Scout leader, all while still at high school.

After Erna finished school, she went to university and graduated with a political science degree. Erna had a lot of ideas about how things should be done in her country, and she wanted to work in a role that could make a difference. All her hard work and experience paid off when she was elected to parliament at the age of 28. Erna Solberg became the leader of her political party in 2004 and was elected prime minister of Norway in 2013 at the age of 52. She was only the second woman to ever hold the position in her country.

Erna has always been open about her learning disorder. As prime minister, she had the option of getting her assistants to write for her, but she wanted to be in control of her own voice and she chose to write her own updates on social media. She stands up for herself when people complain about her spelling and grammar, telling her critics and people all over the world that having dyslexia is nothing to be ashamed of.

Erna's story shows how the experiences you have growing up will inform your beliefs as an adult. Dinner-time discussions with her family helped Erna have an awareness of and passion for helping others. Being a scout leader showed her the value of teamwork and sharing a common vision. And growing up with the challenge of dyslexia taught her to be strong and to fight for what she believes in.

Just like me

Nelson Rockefeller – US vice president

Trevor Watts – Australian MP

Sir Richard Taylor

Special Effects Filmmaker

Born 8 February 1965 • New Zealand

'Students need time and attention to celebrate their uniqueness and to be guided towards a future that endorses and celebrates their differences.'

Sir Richard Taylor

Richard was the type of kid who doodled on the back of his pencil case and daydreamed during exams. He was far more interested in making sculptures and drawing pictures than in traditional academic subjects, and he always knew that he would find success in the creative arts. But first he had to get through school.

Richard and his family had moved from England to a small country town in New Zealand when Richard was an infant. Richard found primary school tough because of his dyslexia, but he was lucky that his high school was accepting of students with learning disabilities. Instead of being forced to fit in with the academic students, Richard was allowed to develop his interest in art and build practical skills like model-making and sculpture, which he was able to use later in life.

Richard followed his dreams of a career in the arts and completed a graphic design course at university. After graduating, Richard and his partner, Tania Rodger, set up a studio called Wētā Workshop in the spare room of their apartment. They made models and puppets and created special effects prosthetics and make-up for TV shows and films in New Zealand. Wētā Workshop became a well-known special effects studio in local productions. Eventually, Richard and Tania moved Wētā Workshop out of their spare room and into a building of its own, and they hired a team of unique and neurodiverse thinkers. They never imagined where they would end up.

One day, Richard received a call from movie director Peter Jackson. Peter was turning a famous book series known as The Lord of the Rings into a spectacular movie trilogy. It was being filmed in New Zealand and Peter asked if Wētā Workshop would be able to help with the special effects. Richard, of course, said yes!

Richard had always been talented, but the work he did with Wētā Workshop for The Lord of the Rings movies earned him four Academy Awards and three BAFTAS in visual effects, make-up and costumes.

Richard has gone on to win many more awards and accolades, including being named New Zealander of the Year in 2012. He was also made a Knight Companion of the New Zealand Order of Merit, turning him into Sir Richard Taylor! Richard achieved all he dreamed of and more. This was all possible because Richard was allowed to focus on the things he was good at.

Just like me

Peggy Stern – Filmmaker

Mads Johan Øgaard – Filmmaker and artist

Dr Maggie Aderin-Pocock

Space Scientist

Born 9 March 1968 • England

'I think people should aspire high and if I don't achieve my ultimate goal – I might never get into space – it doesn't matter, because I will have achieved so much more than if I hadn't tried.'

Dr Maggie Aderin-Pocock

Maggie was born one year before the first moon landing, and she grew up dreaming of space. She would watch TV shows like *Star Trek* and *The Clangers* and hope that one day she would be able to visit the stars, just like her favourite characters.

Maggie's family didn't have a lot of money, but she was a tenacious child and saved up enough money to buy a telescope. Unfortunately, the telescope wasn't very good. But Maggie found a way to get a better one. She saw an advert for a telescope-making class! When Maggie arrived, she was the only young girl in a class of middle-aged men. But she remained determined to make her telescope. Over the following weeks, Maggie learned how to grind special mirrors into lenses, and after months of hard work she had made a beautiful telescope that she could use to see the stars and the craters of the moon.

Maggie was eight when she was diagnosed with dyslexia. She struggled to read and write, and this made her afraid that her dreams would never come true. Maggie had lots of amazing ideas, but she was frustrated because she couldn't find the words to get her amazing ideas onto paper. Often she would sit and sulk at the back of the class. One day, her science teacher asked the class a question. Maggie instantly knew the answer, but when she saw that no one else in the class had put their hand up, she was afraid she must be wrong. The teacher called on her, and to everyone's surprise, Maggie was right!

Maggie realised that if she did well at science, she might one day achieve her dream of going into space. She went to university and studied physics and engineering all the way up to a PhD. Maggie's dad was a huge support and helped her to believe that anything was possible.

Maggie is now a space scientist who builds satellites and telescopes. One of her career highlights was building an instrument for the telescope at the Gemini Observatory in Chile, where she worked for a while. She has done lots of other fun things as a space scientist, like hanging out of aeroplanes to take photographs of missiles going underneath her.

Maggie is also very passionate about science communication. She works as a TV presenter and regularly visits schools to inspire young people with her passion for science and space. She has been so successful as a spokesperson for the importance of science and education that she was awarded a special honour – the Most Excellent Order of the British Empire – by Queen Elizabeth II.

Maggie's dyslexia has helped her to get to where she is today. She pursued the things she was good at – like science and building things – and never stopped reaching for the stars.

Just like me

Dr Matthew H Schneps – Astrophysicist

Dr Wallace Broecker – Geophysicist and climate scientist

Jamie Oliver

Celebrity Chef

Born 27 May 1975 • England

'Being dyslexic or having special needs is not an excuse or reason for you not to prosper. When someone says to you, "Johnny's got dyslexia", you should get down on your knees, shake the child's hand and say, "Well done, you lucky, lucky boy".'

Jamie Oliver

Jamie grew up in the south-east of England, where his mum and dad owned a pub. As a kid, his job was washing the bins, but when he got his very own chef's knife at the age of 8, he started chopping veggies. Soon, he was able to chop veggies better than any of the kitchen staff.

Jamie loved working in the kitchen and he was skilful with his hands, but he found school difficult. His dyslexia greatly affected his schoolwork, and for five years he was placed in a special-needs classroom. Jamie knew that he had to work harder than anyone else, but he still struggled every day. However, he did not let challenges at school stop him from excelling at what he truly loved: cooking.

After finishing school, Jamie enrolled in a catering college to learn how to become a professional chef. For the first time in his life, he started getting top grades. Before long, Jamie had moved on from his family's pub and was working in some of the best restaurants in London. He worked hard and was very skilled, and he was also funny and friendly. He was the type of person that everybody loved to work with.

One day, a TV crew was filming in the restaurant that Jamie was working in. Jamie showed off to the cameras and people loved him! Soon, he had his own cooking show on TV, which launched his career as a celebrity chef. He was known for being fun and down-to-earth.

Jamie remembered what it was like to struggle and feel angry every day, so he used his celebrity profile to help others. He started a not-for-profit restaurant that taught cookery to disadvantaged kids, some of whom were homeless or had other problems. There were 15 trainees in the first year, so Jamie called the restaurant Fifteen. It ran for 17 years and had around 150 graduates, some of whom now head their own restaurants.

Jamie does not see his dyslexia as something to be ashamed of. He calls himself lucky. Jamie believes his dyslexia has helped him succeed because it has given him a unique perspective. He sees problems differently and can find innovative solutions to them. For example, he has written more than 30 cookbooks. But how could he write cookbooks if he'd never even read a book? He recorded himself talking about the recipes and then his receptionist typed up his recordings! His first book made him a millionaire.

All the years that Jamie spent putting in extra effort at school meant that as an adult he works super hard and isn't put off by making mistakes. Once he found his strength – cooking – Jamie was unstoppable.

Just like me

Andrew Dornenburg – Chef

Marco Pierre White – Chef

Jackie French

Author

Born 29 November 1953 • Australia

'Dyslexics who don't give up tend to be very, very good at what we do. Talent is common. Genius is talent plus determination. There's a good chance you're going to have that.'

Jackie French

Jackie has always loved stories. One boring Sunday afternoon, when Jackie was 6 years old and had run out of books to read, she decided to write a book. Jackie was proud of her work and took her book to school. The principal thought Jackie's book was so good that she made a copy of it for every child in the school. After that, Jackie's teacher would let her tell stories to the other children at the end of the day, if the class had behaved themselves.

School wasn't always easy for Jackie, though, because she had dyslexia. She could read quickly in certain formats, but she sometimes had difficulty reading single words on a blackboard.

Her handwriting was almost impossible to read and this combined with her terrible spelling would make her teachers shake their heads in disbelief. Jackie also had dyscalculia and would constantly mix up numbers. Luckily for Jackie, her teachers were more interested in the things that Jackie had to say rather than how messy her work was.

During university and afterwards, Jackie had many jobs: she was a cook, a journalist, a farmer, an assistant for a private detective and even an echidna milker! But Jackie always wanted to be a writer.

When she was 30, Jackie sent her first manuscript to a publisher. She wrote it using an old typewriter from the tip. The letter E wouldn't work, possibly because Jackie's pet wombat, Smudge, would leave droppings on the keyboard. But even though Jackie's story was badly spelled, everyone loved it, and soon it was published into a book.

Jackie has now written more than 200 books for children and adults. One of her most famous is *Diary of a Wombat*. Jackie loves wombats as much as she loves books, and she has many wombats living in her garden along with some possums, echidnas, two handsome roosters and several wallabies.

Jackie believes that if you're dyslexic, the early years of school are often the hardest. You have to learn to learn, and you have to concentrate hard and be determined. Her advice to children with dyslexia is to 'keep at it, because one day you're going to soar'.

Jackie now soars as one of Australia's favourite storytellers. She advocates for children with learning difficulties and she believes that no one should be left behind. Jackie also believes in the power of books to help children learn about the world, inspire them and give them the tools they need for the future they deserve.

Just like me

Tom McLaughlin – Author

Sally Gardner – Author

Dr Fred Epstein

Neurosurgeon

Born 26 July 1937

Died 9 July 2006 • USA

'I decided that if I was going to dream,
I'd reach for the moon. The greater the challenge,
the harder I vowed to work.'

Dr Fred Epstein

Fred stood at the blackboard in his Grade 1 classroom and carefully wrote the words his teacher was telling him. When he was finished, he stepped proudly away from the board. Behind him, the room erupted into laughter. Fred was confused – what was so funny? Then his teacher scolded him for writing every letter E back to front. Fred couldn't see what was wrong, but he didn't like being laughed at.

Fred was born in a small town just outside of New York City and grew up in a family of academic achievers. His father was an important doctor and his mother had a postgraduate degree in social work. Both of Fred's brothers performed well at school, but Fred struggled. He read slowly and mixed up his numbers. Fred found school so difficult that he often pretended to be sick just so he could stay home.

In Grade 5, one of Fred's teachers pulled him aside. 'You got every question on your test paper wrong,' he said to Fred. 'But I know you understand it, so I am going to ask you the questions, and you can just tell me the answers.' Fred got every single question right, and from that day his teacher began to teach him special skills to help with his reading and writing. Fred started to look forward to going to school.

Fred wanted to be a doctor like his dad, but he thought that his reading problem would make that impossible. But Fred had a solution. His aunt was a Grade 1 teacher, and so every weekend Fred would ride his bike to her house, where she would patiently help him with his reading and writing. Slowly, success came and one day, the principal took Fred aside and told him she would write him a letter of recommendation so that he could go to university and become a doctor, just like he had always dreamed.

Fred applied to many different medical schools and was knocked back many times. This was the 1960s and not much was known about dyslexia. All people could see was how much Fred struggled. He was even told he didn't belong at a medical school. But eventually Fred was accepted, and he worked harder and studied longer than any of his classmates did.

Fred went on to become one of the world's most respected and innovative brain surgeons. His dyslexic brain saw solutions where others only saw risks, and he worked with many sick children whose families had been told there was no hope. Fred went on to develop new tools and methods of operating that have saved the lives of many children.

Just like me

Dr Harvey Cushing – Pioneer of neurosurgery

Dr Helen Brooke Taussig – Founder of paediatric cardiology

Cher

Singer and Actor

Born 20 May 1946 • USA

'I think people have to know they're special.'

Cher

Cher was born with the name Cherilyn Sarkisian, but she is so famous that she needs only one name now.

Today, Cher is a successful actor and singer, but she faced a number of challenges growing up. She struggled in school and her teachers always thought she wasn't meeting her potential. In some subjects, she got As and Bs, but mostly she got Ds and Fs. She found it hard to follow along in class when everyone was reading, and often she could not finish her homework in time because she was so slow at reading. Maths felt like a foreign language to her. When she was writing, she would miss letters in the middle of the words, and her hand never worked fast enough to keep up with her brain. Her teachers thought she just didn't study hard enough, and Cherilyn became discouraged.

In the second week of Year 11, Cherilyn walked out of school and never went back. She knew she had lots of potential and just needed to find the right opportunity to show everyone what she was capable of. She enrolled in acting classes in Los Angeles and started calling herself Cher.

It wasn't long before people realised that Cher was destined to succeed. She met a singer called Sonny Bono, which was the start of a very successful partnership. They began to record songs together and co-hosted a popular TV show. Sonny and Cher were also married and had two children. Later, Cher started acting in movies and pursued a solo singing career. She won lots of awards, including an Academy Award, throughout her acting and music career.

One day, Cher was speaking with a doctor about her son, who was experiencing difficulties at school. Cher was shocked when the doctor told her that both she and her son had dyslexia. Sometimes dyslexia can run in families. Suddenly it made sense to Cher why she had always struggled with reading and writing.

Like many people with dyslexia, Cher found ways of adapting. She has excellent memorisation skills, which she used to remember information she was taught at school. She is a slow reader, but this means she pays attention to every word when she reads her film scripts very slowly. And she listens very carefully to what is being said, which means she can remember a lot of information that other people cannot.

Cher is open and honest about her learning difficulty with the millions of fans who follow her, and she has now become an advocate for kids with learning and attention issues.

Cher has been asked if she wishes she didn't have dyslexia, but she said that even though dyslexia has caused her pain, it has made her who she is today.

Just like me

Mireille Mathieu – Singer

Abhishek Bachchan – Actor and producer

Chris Robshaw

Rugby Captain

Born 4 June 1986 • England

'When kids are dyslexic, they need an avenue to be good at something, to be rewarded. You see a lot of dyslexic people going into sport, music or art. For me, that was my escape from the classroom.'

Chris Robshaw

For as long as he could remember, Chris dreamed of playing rugby for England. In the middle of the pitch was where Chris felt alive. It was his happy place and it gave him the strength to deal with other difficulties he was facing.

Chris was only five years old when his father died unexpectedly. In those early years of primary school, Chris had a hard time, and it also became apparent that he was dyslexic. Chris had a lot of anger and energy – he was frustrated at school and sad about his dad.

Playing sports made Chris feel better, and he was very good at them. And when Chris discovered rugby, it gave him the confidence to work harder at school. He was lucky to be sent to a high school that specialised in both sports and dyslexia. Chris had dreaded going to his previous school, especially when teachers would make him stand up and read aloud from a book. But at Chris's new school he was given the support and tools he needed to overcome his reading difficulties. Sometimes that meant staying in at lunchtime to do extra work – which no kid likes – but Chris endured it because he was determined to do well.

Chris had a big supporter in his mum. She would spend most weekends driving him to matches in a car that was always breaking down. Chris was so determined to play as many games as he could, and get as much practice as he could, that sometimes his grandfather and coaches would also need to help drive him to games.

Chris's hard work and determination paid off. In 2012, after years of playing at club level, then national level, Chris Robshaw was chosen as captain of England's national Rugby Union team. Chris led his team in 43 tests, which was more than almost any other player.

Like many dyslexics, Chris is a visual thinker. He will get out onto the pitch and visualise himself performing the passes or tackles he wants to achieve. He is able to mentally practise the plays long before the game even starts.

Years of having to put in extra effort at school and working through lunchtimes prepared him for the challenge of working hard to stay at the top of his rugby game. The little boy who dreamed of playing for his country discovered that, with determination, focus and a lot of hard work, dreams do come true.

Just like me

Samuel Allardyce – Football manager

Kenny Logan – Rugby player

Dr Cathy Foley

Chief Scientist

Born 10 November 1957 • Australia

'It doesn't matter what disability you have, you can navigate the world and solve problems from a different angle – which is such an amazing skill.'

Dr Cathy Foley

As a child, Cathy Foley never could have imagined that she would become Australia's Chief Scientist. Her teachers would never have imagined it either. Cathy was always getting in trouble for her untidy handwriting and terrible spelling. She also had difficulty reading because the words would move around on the page. But Cathy knew there were lots of things she was good at. She was excellent at maths and very clever at finding solutions to problems. She realised that if she could find a solution to a maths problem, she could find a solution for her difficulty with words.

Cathy discovered ways to navigate the early years of school. While it was tough, and she was constantly teased because of her challenges with reading and writing, she went on to develop resilience because of the challenges she faced. Cathy later discovered she had dyslexia when she was in high school, but by then she had already discovered a love of science. She accepted she was not very good at writing, but she knew she was great at lab work, maths and research. Scientists need to be able to think about connections between ideas and look at problems from different angles, and Cathy's difficulty at school had given her plenty of practice at this.

Cathy had also seen her mother solve a different kind of problem. When Cathy was growing up, married mothers like hers were not allowed to work in the New South Wales public service. But Cathy's mum was an architect and she wanted to keep working after she got married and had kids, so she started her own practice. This was quite rare for a woman to do, and it showed Cathy that you can solve problems by being brave and questioning the status quo. Cathy grew up knowing that women had just as much to contribute as men.

Cathy attained a PhD in physics and eventually became the Chief Scientist at CSIRO – the Australian national science agency. She has won numerous awards and her research has led to many important discoveries. Crucially, Cathy focuses on what she is good at rather than what she isn't. She still has trouble with spelling and sometimes has difficulty recognising words, but she is a problem-solver at heart and uses tools such as spellcheck to help her. She also found that working hard on her writing led to huge improvements.

In January 2021, Cathy was appointed as Australia's Chief Scientist. This made her the most senior of all scientists in the country. Cathy provides advice to the prime minister and promotes science to the public. She knows it will be science that solves the problems we face today. Like many others with dyslexia, Cathy found her passion and followed it to great heights. She constantly questions what we know and don't know yet, and always looks for opportunities to make a lasting impact on the world.

Just like me

Dr Carol Greider – Molecular biologist and Nobel Prize Winner

Dr Jacques Dubochet – Molecular biophysicist and Nobel Prize winner

Ingvar Kamprad

IKEA Founder

Born 30 March 1926

Died 27 January 2018 • Sweden

'Creativity and believing in your work is absolutely a necessary part of success.'

Ingvar Kamprad

Ingvar was born in the Swedish province of Småland, where most families, including Ingvar's, were very poor. When Ingvar was only 6, he helped his family make money by selling matches. By the age of 10, Ingvar was riding his bike around town, selling fish, pencils and Christmas decorations to neighbours.

Ingvar was a creative thinker, though he struggled at school and didn't know why. But he studied extra hard and finished school with good grades at the age of 17. His father gave him a small sum of money for doing well, and Ingvar used the money to start a small business that sold things like wallets, watches and belts.

Within five years, Ingvar's business was so successful that he decided to experiment with something new. He sold furniture made from the pale wood of a nearby forest and had it delivered to customers by a fleet of milk trucks. He called his business IKEA. The I and K stood for Ingvar Kamprad, the E stood for Elmtaryd (the farm where Ingvar grew up) and the A stood for Agunnaryd (his village).

Ingvar remembered what it was like growing up poor, so it was important to him that his furniture was affordable. But the people who made the furniture for IKEA said Ingvar was selling their work too cheaply, and they stopped working for him. Ingvar refused to give up and decided he would start designing his own furniture.

One day, Ingvar noticed an employee taking the legs off a table so that it would fit into a customer's car. Ingvar's aptitude for problem-solving and creative thinking kicked in: he realised that if he could make all his furniture fit into a flat box, the customers could put it together at home. It would be easier to transport and would save a lot of money. This was the beginning of the flat-packed furniture design that IKEA is well-known for.

As IKEA's furniture designs grew, Ingvar found he could not remember the codes he was using to identify all the furniture. He discovered the reason he had difficulty with things like number sequences was because he had dyslexia. Like many dyslexics, Ingvar thought in a visual way, so he gave each product a special Swedish name that he could picture and remember. Chairs and desks have male names, while fabric and curtains have female names. The garden furniture is named after Scandinavian islands, while bed and bath items are named after plants and flowers. Ingvar's system was consistent and easy for him to remember even as the product list grew into the thousands.

Ingvar always did things his own way, and he looked for opportunity even in the face of a challenge. IKEA is now one of the most famous stores in the world.

Just like me

Anita Roddick – Founder of The Body Shop

Peter Alexander – Fashion designer

Octavia Spencer

Actor

Born 25 May 1972 • USA

'You have to not see boundaries.
You have to see the sky as the limit
otherwise you will never get off the ground.'

Octavia Spencer

Octavia grew up in a small town with her mum and six brothers and sisters. Octavia's mother raised the children to understand that the only limitations they would face would be the ones they put on themselves.

Her mother's support and positivity was important for Octavia because she had trouble reading and would often mix up her words. She hated being called upon in class to read aloud. But despite this, Octavia was a happy child and didn't think of dyslexia as a disability. She knew she had plenty of skills that the other kids did not. She solved puzzles faster than anyone else and was very clever at problem-solving.

When Octavia was reading, she wasn't always sure what the most important words were, so she paid attention to everything and became extra observant. She found she could grasp concepts better when she heard them, rather than when she was reading them. Octavia began to understand she had a different way of learning to her peers. Despite her reading difficulties, Octavia was so clever that she was tested for entrance into her school's gifted program.

Octavia also had a talent for entertaining people. At school, she would help with the morning announcements and imitate famous actors when doing so. But Octavia dreamed of working behind the camera, too. When she was 16, she discovered a movie was being filmed nearby and visited the set every day asking for a job.

Eventually, Octavia's persistence paid off. They said, 'You're not going to stop, are you?' and gave her a job.

After graduating from university, Octavia began working in TV and movies. This time, she was in front of the camera. Learning scripts with her co-workers was difficult for Octavia because the fear of reading aloud had never left her, but she knew from her studies that she just had to take it slow and persevere. She wasn't going to let something like dyslexia stop her from achieving her goals! Octavia went on to become a successful actor and has won several awards, including an Academy Award.

When she was a child, Octavia loved mystery stories, but being an author of them was something she would never have considered possible. Now, Octavia has written two children's books about a young girl who's a ninja detective. She knew that children who struggle to read, like her, need something exciting to hook them in.

Her mother's words stayed with her forever, and Octavia refused to limit herself or her dreams. So, Octavia never thought of her dyslexia as something that could hold her back.

Just like me

Whoopi Goldberg – Actor

Salma Hayek – Actor

Vincent Fantauzzo

Artist

Born 1977 • Australia

'I talk very openly about being dyslexic because I know there's people out there that are dyslexic; that if they can see what I can do, they can do it as well.'

Vincent Fantauzzo

When Vincent was growing up, he was allowed to do something that most other kids aren't: he could draw and paint on the walls. Vincent's family moved house so many times when he was a child that he had plenty of walls to paint on! He was so talented at art that he could paint realistic holes in the brick wall. You'd almost believe you could step through the hole and into something incredible on the other side.

When Vincent was painting and drawing, he felt confident. But the rest of the time, Vincent was hiding a huge secret. He always knew he wasn't like everyone else – that he saw the world differently from the other kids at school. Where other kids thought in words, Vincent would think in pictures. He struggled with almost all aspects of his schooling: he never did his homework, he avoided tests and he often got into trouble. After failing many subjects, Vincent left school at the very young age of 13.

He worked in various jobs, but he continued to draw and paint in his spare time. Some years later, a friend suggested that Vincent study art at university. Vincent knew it would be a challenge, especially because he hadn't finished high school, but he did it anyway.

During his time at university, Vincent developed his painting skills, but he struggled with the written assignments. One day, he was called in to see the professor. Vincent had been paying other students to write his essays for him, and his professor had caught him. It was finally time for Vincent to confess the secret he had been keeping his entire life: he could not read or write.

The university was very understanding and suggested Vincent get tested for a learning disorder. When he was diagnosed with severe dyslexia, they gave him strategies for dealing with it. Vincent graduated from the Royal Melbourne Institute of Technology and went on to complete a Master of Fine Arts. Later, the man who never finished high school was made an honorary professor.

Vincent views his dyslexia as a gift because of the special way it helps him see the world and the people he is painting. When people look at his portraits, they feel connected to the person, as if they already know the person staring back at them.

Vincent Fantauzzo started by painting on the walls at home. Now, his paintings hang on the walls of galleries all around the country. He has won many prizes for his artworks and become one of Australia's best-loved artists.

Just like me

Robert Rauschenberg – Artist

David Bailey – Photographer

Dame Darcey Bussell

Principal Ballerina

Born 27 April 1969 • England

'Try everything that is out there.
Don't ever believe there is only one path for you.'

Dame Darcey Bussell

One day at school, young Darcey hid away from everyone else. She could hear noises from the other students and the voice of her English teacher, but she stayed quiet and still, hoping no one would find her. Then the door opened a crack and her teacher crouched down. 'The class is almost over, Darcey,' he said kindly. 'It would be nice if you came out of the cupboard.'

Darcey had dyslexia and would do almost anything to avoid classes that involved reading, spelling and numbers. Some of her teachers called her lazy and the other children teased her. But Darcey excelled at other activities like sport, drama and art.

When Darcey was only 5, she began ballet lessons every Saturday morning. She loved it, and dance became an escape for her. At 13, she was accepted into the lower school of the Royal Ballet. Here, dancers would learn classical ballet alongside their academic education.

Most of Darcey's peers had already been at the school for two years, and Darcey realised how far behind the other students she was. Some of the teachers thought she did not belong, and Darcey wondered if she should quit. Her dyslexia even affected her dancing. She would mix up her left and right and would move one way while the rest of the class moved in the other direction.

Darcey's mum told her, 'You can always prove people wrong.' And that is what Darcey did. She was used to being behind, and she knew that perseverance and determination would help her to get better. She worked harder and caught up with her classmates.

Darcey's persistence paid off. At the age of 20, she became the Royal Ballet's principal ballerina. This meant she danced the lead roles. Darcey stayed principal ballerina for almost 20 years and became one of the most popular British dancers of her generation. In 2018, in recognition of Darcey's contribution to dance, she was awarded a Dame (Commander of the Order) of the British Empire by Queen Elizabeth II, and she thereby became Dame Darcey Bussell.

As an adult, Darcey can't hide in a cupboard to avoid the pain of her dyslexia, which still affects her. Since retiring from the Royal Ballet, Darcey performs on TV, yet she finds reading scripts difficult. She is often asked to sign things for fans, but she will sometimes freeze in fear. But Darcey sees her dyslexia as a small blessing because it helped her find her strength in dance and showed her that there are many paths to success other than academic grades.

Just like me

Meryl Davis – Olympic ice skater

Elizabeth Arifen and Charlotte Edmonds – Choreographers

Steven Spielberg

Filmmaker

Born 18 December 1946 • USA

'You are not alone, and while you will have dyslexia for the rest of your life, you can dart between the raindrops to get where you want to go. It will not hold you back.'

Steven Spielberg

Being the new kid at school can be hard. For Steven, this was a regular occurrence. Steven's family moved around a lot to follow his dad's work, which meant Steven and his three sisters moved between schools in different states. At each new school Steven faced the same problems. He was a slow reader, and he was embarrassed to stand in front of the class and read aloud. His teachers thought he was lazy, and he was bullied and teased by the other kids. He had no name for what was wrong with him; he just knew he hated school.

Steven's escape was making movies. From an early age, he made adventure films using a camera his dad gave him. By the time he was 15, he had won his first award for a film called *Escape to Nowhere*.

While Steven dreaded going to school, he loved making movies – he could communicate not only with words, but also with pictures. He realised the power of making movies when he cast one of his bullies as the hero in one of his films. Steven never forgot how mean the boy had been, but he was able to convert the bully to a friend by placing him in front of the camera.

Steven's parents encouraged him to keep making movies, and he dedicated much of his free time to filmmaking. But despite this, Steven's applications to study film at university were rejected – three times! Despite his other successes, Steven's grades were just too low.

As an adult, Steven not only directs movies but has also helped write and produce them as well. It may take him twice as long as others to read a script, but he spends extra time lingering over the words, and he can remember details that other people might not notice. And like many other dyslexics, Steven has an eye for detail while also being able to see the big picture. Many of his films have won awards and he has directed many blockbusters, including *Jurassic Park*, *E.T.* and *Jaws*. Steven also formed a successful movie studio called Dreamworks SKG, which has made films like *Trolls*, *Kung Fu Panda* and *Captain Underpants*.

Steven wasn't diagnosed with dyslexia until he was in his sixties. He said it was like finding the final piece of a puzzle! Having dyslexia finally explained why he took such a long time to read things and why he had struggled so much at school.

Steven's path to success wasn't easy. He faced challenges including bullying and rejection. But he never gave up on doing what he loved, and he found creative solutions to overcome the obstacles in his way. Eventually, that took him all the way to Hollywood.

Just like me

Guy Ritchie – Filmmaker

Søren Kragh Jacobsen – Filmmaker

Anne Burke

Supreme Court Chief Justice

Born 3 February 1944 • USA

'Dyslexia is just a different way of perceiving the world. It's helped me gain problem-solving skills and take risks that others might never consider.'

SPECIAL

Anne Burke

Anne always knew she would never be an A student. She wasn't even a B student. She had difficulties with reading, writing and maths all through school, but that was just the way it was. She read and wrote from right to left, and her teachers constantly reminded her she was doing it backwards, but no one told her off and no one told her to try harder.

Instead, Anne's parents encouraged her to do the thing she was good at: sport. Anne loved all sports, from basketball and running to swimming and tap dance. She also enjoyed working with kids, so she became a camp counsellor during her summer breaks in high school.

Anne discovered she had dyslexia while she was at college. Now everything made sense: dyslexia was at the root of all the mix-ups at school, like writing her name backwards and taking two or three times as long as the other children to read and comprehend written words.

From her experiences, Anne knew that children just need to be given an opportunity to find something they are good at. She decided to become a gym teacher and to dedicate her time to working with children with special needs. She knew that all children have the same dreams: to feel they are part of something, to achieve and to win.

By the age of 23, Anne had helped convince her local district to hold the Chicago Special Olympics, so people in her area with disabilities could compete in sports events. Following its success, Anne took the Special Olympics nationwide with 2,000 athletes from

26 states. Anne couldn't have imagined how successful this would be. Fifty years later, the Special Olympics are now a global event that are held in almost 200 countries and help to change the way people with mental and physical disabilities are viewed.

Anne never stopped thinking of other ways to help people with disabilities, and she soon realised she could do even more if she was involved in making the laws that protected and supported them. So, Anne enrolled in law school. Due to her dyslexia, Anne found the curriculum challenging, but she discovered she is an auditory learner, which means she absorbs and remembers things better by listening rather than reading.

After graduating, Anne opened a small law office that helped families and vulnerable children. And following years of hard work and fighting for those in need, she became a judge in the state Supreme Court.

As a Supreme Court Justice, Anne is known for her empathy. From her own difficulties at school to her work with children and adults throughout her life, she has an enormous understanding of other people's struggles and fights for those without power.

Just like me

Jeffrey H Gallet – Court judge

Crispian Wilson – Diplomat

John Hoke

Designer

Born 10 October 1964 • USA

'I came to this idea that my dyslexia wasn't actually a burden – it was a gift because it made me look at the world differently.'

John Hoke

John felt emotional as he watched the TV coverage of Allyson Felix racing around the track of the 2016 Olympic 400-metre final. Allyson was a six-time gold medallist, and she was wearing shoes that had been specially designed by John to enhance her unique running style over the curve of the track.

John is the Chief Design Officer for Nike, one of the world's largest sportswear companies. He leads a team of over 1,000 designers and has input in every shoe that is created. Communication is an important part of his role: he connects people from 30 departments across multiple continents. But when John stands in front of a group of people, he cannot read a speech word for word – his brain does not work that way. He has had to develop different ways of working and communicating.

John was diagnosed with dyslexia early in life. Though he struggled at school, especially with reading and writing, he was well-supported by his family and had access to specialist help. John discovered that his dyslexia brought with it one of his greatest talents – the ability to think of the world in pictures. John thought of drawing as his first language, and it was how he best communicated with others. While other students worked diligently on essay writing, John would spend most of his class time carefully designing and drawing a title and graphics instead.

John was also interested in how the equipment that athletes used, like shoes, helped to make them successful. He would cut open his old sneakers to see what was inside because he was curious about how they were made. One summer, while he was floating around a pool on an inflatable raft, he thought about how comfortable it would be to have a raft-like cushion on your feet as you ran. He went inside and doodled a picture of his idea and then sent it to the president of Nike. Before long, he received a reply in the mail (together with a free T-shirt and pair of shoes) that said, 'When you're old enough, can you come work for me?'

Now that John runs the design department at Nike, he can still sketch and doodle more than he writes. John has discovered that he listens better when his hands are busy, so he is always drawing – and sometimes that is when he has his best ideas.

John's dyslexia helps him see the world differently, which has given him a creative edge. From designing his first shoe as a child to watching Allyson Felix take home an Olympic medal wearing shoes he helped design, John remains excited about seeing his ideas come to life.

Just like me

Peter Alexander – Fashion designer

Jørn Utzon – Architect

Sir Richard Branson

Entrepreneur

Born 18 July 1950 • England

'If anyone ever puts you down for having dyslexia, don't believe them. Being dyslexic can actually be a big advantage, and it has certainly helped me.'

Sir Richard Branson

From a young age, Richard came up with innovative ways to make money. He had lots of good ideas, but plenty that didn't work, too.

One year, Richard tried growing Christmas trees, but he discovered rabbits ate all the seedlings. Another year, he convinced his dad to spend a weekend building a large cage for budgerigars, which Richard planned to breed. After a while, his parents got tired of taking care of the birds and let them fly away. But Richard did not let these failures stop him. He simply moved on to his next big idea.

Even though Richard had lots of creative ideas, some of his teachers thought he was stupid and lazy. They didn't understand that Richard had dyslexia and that this made it difficult for him to grasp a concept if it didn't interest him. Richard was often punished at school. One day, his principal told Richard he would either end up in prison or become a millionaire.

Richard knew which option he wanted, so at the age of 15 he left school, moved to London and started his first business – his own magazine. London in the 1960s was full of creative people just like Richard. Soon he met a lot of musicians, which inspired his next business idea – a music company that Richard called Virgin. Before long he had music stores around the globe and a recording studio where famous bands came to record their music.

Richard didn't stop thinking of new ideas, regardless of whether his previous ideas were successful or failed. Being dyslexic, he is innovative and adventurous, and he sees opportunities where other people might not. Richard grew his business to include an airline and a mobile phone company. In recent years, Virgin has built a rocket that may soon fly people into space.

As Richard gets older, he has learned more about dyslexia and how his learning difference affects him. He has adapted his work style to focus on what he is good at, and he delegates jobs that he is not good at to people who are skilled in those areas. Richard's dyslexia also helped him understand the importance of having simple communication. He has made sure that his companies have easy-to-read documents and contracts without big, technical words in them.

Richard has turned a lot of good ideas into great successes. He believes he would not have been as successful if he didn't have dyslexia because it has taught him to view the world differently from other people, to focus on the things he is good at, and to look forward rather than dwelling on past failures.

Just like me

Kerry Stokes AC – Media mogul

Steve Jobs – Founder of Apple

Dame Agatha Christie

Author

Born 15 September 1890

Died 12 January 1976 • England

'Writing and spelling were always terribly difficult for me. My letters were without originality. I was ... an extraordinarily bad speller and have remained so.'

Dame Agatha Christie

As a young girl, Agatha would play the piano to herself for hours. She was very talented and could have become a professional pianist, but she was extremely shy and did not like to play in front of strangers. She did like to watch them, though. She learned a lot about people and the things they did when they thought no one was watching.

Unlike her older brother and sister, who had been sent away to school, Agatha was taught lessons at home by her father. She was a very curious child and had taught herself to read at the age of 4. Despite being a passionate reader, she had great difficulty with numbers and was terrible at spelling. But with her father's help, she soon began writing little poems and stories.

Agatha's father died suddenly when she was 11. Without her father to teach her, Agatha was sent away to school, first in England and then in France, where she struggled badly. She left school when she was 15 and returned to England to live with her mother.

Agatha got married at the age of 22 in 1913, the year before World War I began. When her husband was away at war, she volunteered at a hospital with the Red Cross. She absorbed interesting information from everything she did in her life. Her work in the hospital pharmacy taught her all about poisons, which later came in handy for her writing!

Agatha kept writing her stories. Her first short stories had been rejected by magazines and her first novel was rejected by six publishers. But by the time she was 30, she had a detective novel published. Its main character was inspired by soldiers Agatha had helped to treat while volunteering.

Agatha collected lots of interesting details from her adventures over the years, such as travelling to Egypt with her mother, learning to surf in Hawaii and exploring archaeological digs with her husband – and used them in her novels. She would write the ideas down in a notebook. Sometimes Agatha kept five notebooks at the same time!

Agatha always had difficulty with spelling, but she found clever solutions to get her stories onto the page. Sometimes she would use a dictaphone to record her stories, while at other times a secretary would type them up for her.

Agatha used her natural curiosity and talent for observation and storytelling to write more than 60 novels. She is one of the bestselling authors of all time and known as the Queen of Mystery. Her books have sold over 4 billion copies around the world, in more than 100 languages, and some have been made into movies, TV series and plays.

Just like me

Pip Williams – Author

Catherine Deveny – Author

Alex Edmondson

Olympic Cyclist

Born 22 December 1993 • Australia

'Dream big. You really never know what is around the corner!'

Alex Edmondson

When the first Harry Potter movie was released in 2001, Alex was secretly relieved. He could finally find out what all the fuss was about. His friends had been reading the books, but Alex had dyslexia and a big book like *Harry Potter and the Philosopher's Stone* seemed impossible to read.

Alex dreaded reading aloud as well as reading privately. The other kids at school laughed at him when he was asked to read to the class. He was also the last kid in his class to get his pen licence. He felt embarrassed when he was pulled out of class to see a special teacher, and he was overwhelmed by all the extra homework. Every birthday when Alex blew out the candles on his cake, he made the same wish: he wanted to be a 'normal' kid.

Alex's parents were always by his side, encouraging him when he wanted to give up and motivating him to show dyslexia that he was the boss. They found him a new school with great support, where he learned he was different but just as capable as other kids.

There was something else about Alex that made him different: he had a very special life goal. Alex wanted to win an Olympic medal in the Australian cycling team. He knew that earning a place on the Olympic team would require the same dedication he put into his schoolwork. Luckily, Alex knew how to work hard.

When Alex was 17, he won two gold medals at the Junior Track Cycling World Championships in Russia. Then, in the same year, he was chosen for the Australian team and flew to Kazakhstan to race in the Track Cycling World Cup. Someone played a prank on him and told him that all new team members needed to give a speech. Alex loved cycling so much he talked to a room full of people for 14 minutes before everyone burst out laughing. But everyone agreed that this was such a good way to learn about the young riders that they decided to keep it as a tradition.

In 2012, when Alex was 18, he was selected for the Australian Olympic cycling team, making him one of the youngest riders ever chosen. Alex was the fifth member of the team, so he did not get to ride when the Australian team made the final. He stood next to the track with tears running down his face, happy that his team was racing but sad that he was not riding.

Four years later, he was selected to go to the 2016 Olympics in Rio de Janeiro. He was part of the men's team that broke a world record and went on to win an Olympic silver medal.

Alex still races, but he wants to be remembered as a good cyclist and a true sportsperson. He remembers what it was like to receive support when he was young and he is now very involved in volunteering to motivate young people. Alex might have once hated going to school and reading aloud, but now he attends schools to encourage students to set goals and strive to be their best.

Just like me

Sir Steve Redgrave – Olympic rower

Greg Louganis – Olympic diver

Swedish Royal Family

King Carl Gustaf XVI

Born 30 April 1946 • Sweden

Crown Princess Victoria

Born 14 July 1977 • Sweden

Prince Carl Philip

Born 13 May 1979 • Sweden

'When even our prince has dyslexia, perhaps [children] won't feel so isolated in the classroom and will go on to make progress at school.'

– Prince Carl Philip

Swedish Royal Family

'What do you want to be when you grow up?' a teacher once asked little Carl Gustaf. 'I'm going to be king,' he replied.

Carl Gustaf did grow up to be the King of Sweden, just as he always knew he would. Growing up, he had access to things that other kids could only dream of, but he did not get the educational support that he needed to manage his dyslexia.

When Carl Gustaf was Crown Prince of Sweden, he was privately educated at home and then at boarding school. Few people knew that Carl Gustaf had difficulties with spelling and reading until he visited a copper mine as part of his royal duties when he was in his late twenties. He was asked to sign his name on a rock wall, but to his embarrassment, he misspelled it. It wasn't until many years later that he addressed his dyslexia publicly, admitting that as a child he didn't get the help he needed, even though he was a prince.

Carl Gustaf's children, Crown Princess Victoria, Princess Madeleine and Prince Carl Philip, have also been diagnosed with dyslexia. Prince Carl Philip kept his difficulties a secret for many years. Crown Princess Victoria was bullied at school and her classmates would laugh when she had to read aloud.

But Prince Carl Philip and Crown Princess Victoria have used their experiences to change the way others look at people with disabilities.

After messing up an important speech at the Swedish Sports Gala one year, Prince Carl Philip was ridiculed in the national papers.

But instead of hiding away, he went back to the Sports Gala and did another speech the following year. This time he talked about his dyslexia and how important it was for him to confront his difficulties. He also reminded everyone, including the media, that bullying is never acceptable.

Crown Princess Victoria has also used her position in the public eye to talk about the difficulty she had growing up, hoping to raise awareness and understanding of the condition she and her family share with the hundreds of thousands of other people with dyslexia in Sweden.

In 2022, Prince Carl along with Princess Beatrice of York, who also lives with dyslexia, opened the first World Dyslexia Assembly in Stockholm. The Prince and Princess spoke of their own journeys with dyslexia and explained that the Assembly will contribute to empowering dyslexic thinking. Together, they will help work towards a more inclusive society, where difference and uniqueness are celebrated.

The experiences of the Swedish royal family show us that even royalty struggle sometimes. Their experiences remind us that dyslexia does not discriminate, even if people and the media are sometimes quick to do so. They also show us that it is important to speak up and speak out.

Just like me

Her Royal Highness Princess Beatrice of York

Prince Harry, Duke of Sussex

Reyn Guyer

Inventor

Born 1935 • USA

'My learning disabilities pushed me to discover talents that I wasn't aware of having.'

Reyn Guyer

Growing up in Minnesota in the 1940s, Reyn loved the outdoors and always preferred to be outside playing sports rather than inside, where there might be books.

Reyn's dyslexia would not be diagnosed for many years, and he had lots of difficulties with his reading and writing. Yet, like many dyslexics, Reyn's challenges forced him to discover his other talents. He was a great artist and could think creatively and innovatively. By the time he was 10, Reyn had already redesigned the one indoor game that he enjoyed playing: Monopoly. On Reyn's version, there were more opportunities to hit the jackpot!

Reyn always tried to approach things from a different angle, which meant he had creative ideas. When Reyn was a young man, he designed advertising campaigns. One day, when he was working on a promotion for tins of shoe polish, he created a game where people had to cross from one side of a large, life-sized board to the other. He gathered a group of secretaries and accountants to try the game, and as they tried to cross the board they were all laughing and falling and winding up in a tangle. Reyn knew he was onto something. He worked with a game designer and an artist to perfect the concept and they eventually produced Twister – a game almost everyone reading this book has likely played or heard of.

Reyn believed in breaking rules. His success in inventing games came from a simple question that he asked himself: 'What happens if?' In 1969, Reyn broke another rule – 'Don't throw balls in the house' – when he invented a soft foam ball that could be thrown indoors without causing damage. That foam ball was the first Nerf ball, and it became so popular there are now Nerf footballs, Nerf ping pong, Nerf guns and even Nerf archery sets.

Not all of Reyn's inventions were instantly successful. He said he had 'a lot of turkeys' over the years – games that never made it to production. Even Twister wasn't popular at first, as people thought it was too scandalous to buy. But Reyn has never let setbacks like these stop him from trying again.

Reyn didn't learn he was dyslexic until he was an adult. His wife and daughter also have dyslexia and together they started Winsor Learning, a company that trains teachers to help children with learning difficulties.

In 1986, Reyn was inducted into the Hasbro Inventors Hall of Fame. Since then, he has continued to use his creative and innovative brain to invent new toys and games.

Just like me

Ky Michealson – Inventor of rocket-powered vehicles

Dr Ursula Kelly – Scientist and inventor

Erin Brockovich

Activist

Born 22 June 1960 • USA

'Life is full of challenges, whether you are learning disabled or not. It's how you handle those challenges.'

Erin Brockovich

One day, when Erin was a little girl, she stood in her classroom and listened sadly while the other girls giggled at her. Erin's teacher had called her 'stupid' in front of the whole class. But Erin knew she wasn't stupid. She could learn – just not in the way they wanted to teach her.

A few years later, a different teacher pulled Erin aside. Erin had failed yet another test, but the teacher wanted to try something new. She tore up the test paper and threw it in the bin. Then she began asking Erin the test questions. When Erin was talking to her teacher rather than staring at a test paper, she could think of all the answers. She got an A+. From that day, things changed for Erin. She realised she was smart and that she could answer test questions. Eventually, her self-esteem grew.

Erin wasn't diagnosed with dyslexia until she was an adult, but she knew that she had to work extra hard in school. This taught her many lessons that helped her later in life. She became determined and strong-willed. She taught herself strategies that would help her understand and then remember information, and knowing she needed to seek out extra support made her resourceful. She had learned that she needed to take responsibility for her own learning and actions.

Erin also remembered what it was like feeling helpless and overwhelmed, and she wanted to help others. This was something that Erin put into practice when she became a legal clerk. This job involved reading and taking notes on thousands and thousands of pages of medical records and legal documents. It was the type of job that as a child she never would have believed she could do. But being dyslexic helped Erin with this task. She was a slow and careful reader, but she had also taught herself to be meticulous and to notice things that other people might skim over.

For one particular case, Erin spent hours and hours reading. She eventually found a link between families who were getting sick and a big gas and electric company that was polluting the local water. It was a very important discovery and the company had to pay hundreds of millions of dollars to the sick families. Later, a movie was made about Erin's discovery.

Erin has kept fighting against big companies that are damaging the environment. She is also an advocate for kids with learning disorders. She believes that even if you have dyslexia, you are so much more than your disability. Erin believes a label shouldn't limit who you want to be and what you think you can do. It certainly never stopped her.

Just like me

David Boies – Attorney

Professor David Schoenbrod – Environmental law pioneer

Charles 'Pete' Conrad

Astronaut

Born 2 June 1930

Died 8 July 1999 • USA

'If you can't be good, be colourful.'

CONRAD

Charles 'Pete' Conrad

Pete had a love of flying from an early age. After his first plane ride at the age of 5, he knew he wanted to become a pilot. But there would be challenges ahead for Pete.

Pete was born into a wealthy family in Philadelphia, where Pete, his parents and two siblings lived in a large house with servants. But by the time he was 12, his family had lost all their savings and Pete's father had abandoned them.

Pete still attended the elite school that his father and grandfather had gone to. But although Pete was bright, clever with his hands, and able to pull apart and rebuild machinery with ease, he struggled with his schoolwork. Dyslexia was poorly understood in the 1940s and most of Pete's teachers thought he was lazy.

One day, Pete's mum came home to find him crying in his room. He had just been told he had failed Year 11 and his school would not let him return the following year. 'I'm so sorry,' he told his mum. 'I can't keep my eyes on the page. I get a headache when I look at the words – they all just run together. Am I stupid?' Pete's mother said that he wasn't and found him a new school, where the teachers helped him with his dyslexia.

Pete still wanted to be a pilot. His family had no money for him to learn to fly, so Pete did odd jobs at a nearby airfield. He mowed lawns, changed tyres and swept up in return for rides in the planes as a passenger. He loved everything about aeroplanes, and he learned how they worked and how to fix them.

When Pete was 16, he helped to fix a local pilot's broken plane. In return, she gave him flying lessons. Pete was a talented pilot and earned his pilot's licence before he even finished high school.

Just as Pete had taught himself to pull apart and put machinery back together, he taught himself how to cope with his dyslexia. He took a systematic approach to learning, knowing there were steps he needed to follow and that things had to be done in a particular order. Pete also had a cheeky sense of humour, which helped him not take problems too seriously.

Soon after university, Pete was accepted into the US Navy and trained as a test pilot and flight instructor. Pete's life changed again after he was asked to apply to the NASA astronaut program. By the age of 39, he was commander of Apollo 12, which was the second mission to land on the moon.

Pete not only became a pilot but he also got to fly all the way to the moon! He was the third man to walk on the moon and is regarded as one of the best pilots of his generation.

Just like me

Lawrence Schneider – NASA engineer

Sir Jackie Stewart – Racing car driver

Dr Willem Kolff

Medical Pioneer

Born 14 February 1911

Died 11 February 2009 • Netherlands

'Whenever I see a problem, I try to reduce it to simple terms. If the problem is very complicated, I look at whether or not there is a simple component to it. And if the simple component is an important part, I take that first.'

B

Dr Willem Kolff

Willem was born in the Netherlands and was the eldest of five children. Their father was a doctor and Willem always knew that he wanted to follow in his footsteps.

Dyslexia wasn't known about when Willem was growing up. He struggled at school and he was constantly punished for his poor reading and writing skills. But Willem's father knew that his son had other strengths.

Willem was a tinkerer and gifted at making things with his hands. So every Saturday afternoon, his dad sent him to have carpentry lessons to develop his skills. These lessons were crucial in helping Willem learn how to build things and understand how they worked.

Despite his difficulty reading and writing, Willem persisted with his dream to go to medical school. With a lot of hard work, he graduated in 1938 and became a doctor. He got a job as an assistant in the medical department and began inventing his first machine, a cuff that would help patients with poor circulation.

One day, a young man suffering from kidney failure came into the hospital where Willem worked. The man's kidneys could not remove all the toxins and poisons from his blood and he died. Willem knew that if he could figure out a way to extract the toxins from the blood of people suffering kidney failure, they might survive. So he began tinkering and building machines.

Not many people would think of making an artificial kidney using parts from an old car, an enamel bath, a wooden drum and cellophane sausage skins. But Willem had spent many years studying how machines worked and was able to use his special brain to see how all these strange parts could be used together.

From this, Willem created the first haemodialysis machine, which could cleanse the toxic blood from a sick patient and return the cleaned blood to the body. In 1945, he saved his first patient with this machine.

After World War II, Willem continued his studies in the Netherlands. He gave away free dialysis machines to researchers around the world and encouraged them to keep working on them.

In 1950, Willem and his family moved to America, where he was able to focus on his new goal: to invent a heart-lung machine. Willem's new machine enabled surgeons to perform open-heart surgery on a patient for the very first time. He also spent many years developing an implantable artificial heart, an artificial eye and even an artificial ear.

Willem's inventions have helped save or prolong the lives of many millions of people around the world. His teachers may have never believed in his dream to go to medical school, but through his curiosity, innovation and determination, Willem became a genius of 20th-century medicine.

Just like me

Dr John B Goodenough – Chemist and Nobel Prize winner

Dr George M Church – Science pioneer

Jade Wheeler

Student Crusader

Born 22 July 2005 • Australia

'Standing up for yourself is courageous and important, but standing up for others combines courage and compassion.'

Jade Wheeler

Jade Wheeler's name might not be as well-known as some others in this book, but you may know Jade's name in the future. She is working hard to help children with dyslexia in Australia.

Jade was in Grade 1 when it became obvious that she had difficulties with her reading and writing. Dyslexia ran in her family, so her parents knew she would need help with her learning.

By Grade 3, Jade was talking to her classmates about dyslexia and how it affected her. When the other students understood what Jade was going through, they were less likely to tease and bully her.

In Grade 6, Jade started The Lightbulb Club, a special group for kids struggling with literacy. She was given an award for courage and resilience.

In Year 7, she wrote to the principal about her struggles with dyslexia. Only a few of her teachers knew much about dyslexia or how to teach dyslexic kids. It is not compulsory for trainee teachers to learn about dyslexia and other learning disabilities, which means that many teachers do not know how to work with students who learn differently.

Outside of school, Jade was busy with another passion: ballet. It has become a huge part of who she is, and she believes it has helped her survive the challenges of being dyslexic.

By the time Jade reached high school, she was passionate about teachers being trained to work with kids who have dyslexia and other learning disabilities. For a school project, Jade wrote about the need for teachers to be taught how to identify and then teach students with dyslexia. She sent her project to four politicians and the vice-chancellors of every Western Australian university with a teaching course.

At age 14, Jade was interviewed on the radio and written about in newspaper articles because she had begun lobbying politicians to make sure that all teachers in Australia are trained to recognise and help children with dyslexia.

Jade doesn't plan to stop there. When she has achieved this goal, Jade will be lobbying the government to provide more funding for families who spend thousands of dollars getting the help they need for their children, such as the costs of diagnosis, testing, tutoring and speech therapy.

Recently, Jade has started mentoring school children with dyslexia. She visits them regularly and shares strategies to help them cope with the challenges that dyslexia presents. Jade's passion to educate and help others is an inspiration to everyone. Along with other young advocates, Jade is working to change how people view dyslexia, encouraging others to see it as a unique set of skills and challenges.

Just like me

Mo, Evie and Otis Maslin Foundation

Georgia Ryan – Youth ambassador

Resources

There are lots of organisations that can help you if you'd like to know more about dyslexia, and if you're looking for support online or locally. The following organisations are a good place to start.

Australian Dyslexic Association

A not-for-profit association concerned with well-being, identification and educational intervention of those who struggle with spoken and written language.

dyslexiaassociation.org.au

Code REaD Dyslexia Network

A national not-for-profit organisation to raise awareness and support Australians with dyslexia.

codereadnetwork.org

Dyslexia Support Australia

A support and information site for children and adults, offering resources for teachers and parents.

www.dyslexiasupportservices.com.au

Dyslexia Victoria Support

A community group for evidence-based education for literacy difficulties, run by volunteers and supported by allied health professionals.

https://dyslexiavictriasupport.com

SPELD Victoria

Provides Specific Learning Difficulties service delivery, information, advocacy and awareness raising in the Victoria community.

speldvic.org.au

Dyslexia NSW

Offers a range of tailored, comprehensive support services and advice for both children and adults with dyslexia.

www.dyslexiansw.com.au

SPELD NSW

A not-for-profit organisation offering support, assistance and advice to children and adults with specific learning difficulties, their families, tutors, teachers and schools.

https://www.speldnsw.org.au

Dyslexia QLD support group

Provides dyslexia screening services.

dyslexiaqueensland.com

SPELD QLD

A not-for-profit organisation supporting all Queenslanders experiencing learning differences to realise their full potential in all circumstances.

www.speld.org.au

Red Apple Dyslexia Association SA

A not-for-profit organisation supporting people with dyslexia and their families, community and teacher awareness.

dyslexiasa.org

SPELD SA

A not-for-profit organisation providing advice and services to the community including educational training, parent workshops, educational consultations, psychological assessments, tutoring, literacy intervention programs, library and bookshop.

speldsa.org.au

Dyslexia-SPELD Foundation, Perth

An independent not-for-profit organisation that provides a range of clinical and literacy services for individuals with persistent learning difficulties and disorders.

dsf.net.au

Canberra Learning and Development Centre

Provides direct, explicit instruction for students struggling with reading, spelling, writing and mathematics.

canberralearningand developmentcentre.com.au

Dear Dyslexic Foundation

Offers young people and adults with learning disabilities a platform to share their lived experience of dyslexia and other learning disabilities.

deardyslexic.com

AUSPELD

(Australian Federation of Specific Educational Learning Difficulties Associations)

AUSPELD represents all states and territory SPELD Associations.

auspeld.org.au

affirm press

Published and Distributed in India by Scholastic India Pvt. Ltd.
First published by Affirm Press in 2022
Boon Wurrung Country
28 Thistlethwaite Street
South Melbourne VIC 3205
affirmpress.com.au

NATIONAL LIBRARY OF AUSTRALIA
A catalogue record for this book is available from the National Library of Australia

ISBN: 978-93-5471-919-6

Cover and internal design © Affirm Press
Typeset in Gotham and Aloha March.

First edition: 2022
This reprint edition: July, 2024

Printed in India at Sai Printo Pack Pvt. Ltd.